"Empowering You to Love Yourself, by Suzanne Harrill, is easy reading with universal appeal. The acorn analogy reflects the truth about the innate goodness of all people. Throughout the book, Suzanne provides the tools for moving people from the "niceness" of external validation to the most empowering and esteeming "leap" one can ever make, that of internal validation. Suzanne warmly communicates her deep sense of spirituality and contribution through her writing. I find myself listening to my "innerself," a joyful experience that I want many others to experience also."

Sandi Redenback, Esteem Seminar Programs and Publications-Davis, CA, Consultant, Teacher Staff Development Trainer and Author of *Self-Esteem: The Necessary Ingredient for Success*, and *Innovative Discipline: Managing Your Own Flight Plan*

"This is firstly an honest book, written by someone who speaks openly about her life experiences. Partly because of that, I find it to be an inspiring book, one that helps me sort and deepen what I know about my own life experiences. It especially helps me know about loving and, alas, still yet failing completely to love myself."

Merrill Harmin, Founder, Inspiring Strategy Institute

"Empowering you to Love Yourself is wonderful! I was particularly touched by her description of the powerlessness that is felt when someone is negative, critical or verbally abusive. In *Empowering You to Love Yourself* you will learn the tools to clear away the unwanted patterns and behaviors by learning to be who you really are...a shining essence of spirit in physical form."

Dolores Ehrlich, Editor: *Self-Esteem Today*

"An easily read, thorough guide to healing our past and enhancing our self-esteem. Suzanne Harrill has given us the basic steps in finding out who we really are and in learning to accept and love what we find"

Betty Hatch, Past President of the National Council for Self-Esteem and founder of La Belle Outreach Foundation

This book is dedicated to:

My dear husband, Rodney A. Harrill

I thank the following people for
helping create this book:
Julie Hills, Kevin Kauffman, Dale Logan

A special thank you to Diane Langley
for all the proofing and editing.

Book design and cover by Lightbourne Images
300 Sheridan, Ashland, Oregon 97520
1-800-697-9833

Table of Contents

Contents continued

Introduction

In this book I hope to give you simple ways to love yourself. There are not many examples, mainly information. Those of you who would like to know more would benefit from reading my first book, *You Could Feel Good.*

Being trained as a marriage and family therapist, I have found it useful to look at yourself within the context of the family you were raised in (family of origin) and the family or marriage you now live in as an adult. Those of you who have the experience of being single, look at yourself in the context of the place you work. Both your current relationships at home and work have elements in common with your family of origin.

I also think it is of value to notice and become aware of the unconscious parts of yourself. To empower you, this shadow side needs to be transformed into the light of understanding. When you work on your shadow, you work towards perceiving your life more and more clearly. I believe we are all on a spiritual journey towards being totally aware.

Let me illustrate with an area I am learning to bring into the light. One of my secrets is that I can lose my power if someone is negative, critical, or verbally abusive towards me. Because I do not come from that intention, I can often deny that anything negative is going on and simply experience many bodily sensations, such as a knot in my stomach and a feeling of wanting to hide and be by myself. In sharing with you part of my shadow side that I am bringing into the light, I hope to motivate your inner healing on your journey to wholeness.

We each perceive the world through the filters of our own consciousness. Whether the outer world perceives our circumstances the same way we do or not, we can only begin to heal from where we are at the moment that we become conscious of needing to heal any emotional dysfunction that is blocking our well-being. As I said earlier, I can deny that anything negative is happening because it is not blatant abuse, such as someone who has undergone the pain and agony of incest or physical abuse. However, that denial will inhibit and block my journey to wholeness.

Being trained as a therapist, I was exposed to healing my present by looking at my family of origin patterns and behaviors. After graduate school, I continued my education of myself by taking workshops, reading self-help books, writing in a journal, and being in therapy. As I continually worked on myself for many years, some patterns did not seem to go away, even though I was taking risks and positively changing many parts of my life. My power issues were the most unconscious. In this area I was the most confused and the least prepared to understand what was going on when I was in a power struggle with someone.

To give you a recent example, a person who sells my books said she would not pay one of the orders I had sent because she had no record of it being delivered. My first response was to feel powerless and that I must be wrong. I could not verbalize anything to support myself. Many times during my life I have backed off when a dominant person insists they are right and I am wrong or wants their way. Being the adult that I am now, I knew I did nothing wrong and that I must stand up for myself. When I hung up the phone, I did feel taken advantage of, which gave me the energy to go back over my last year's records, find the UPS slip, track down when it was delivered and who had signed for it. In this case, it was fairly easy. It was difficult for me, however, to call the woman back and tell her the details which proved I was right. I felt short of breath and anxious as I dialed the number, just as I did when I had done something wrong as a child. It was helpful to talk to myself in a warm and kind manner, saying things such as, "You can do it, you haven't done anything wrong." In that way, I could complete the call.

I have found that it takes very little for me to feel powerless. And I emphasize that it is what I am feeling, not what an outside observer would see. Clues to why I have this response are learned by looking at communication patterns, parenting patterns, and problem-solving patterns in my family of origin. The responsibility for healing and changing these patterns resides within me today.

At times it was difficult for me to look to my family of origin as contributing to some of my problems because it was usually little things from my childhood that were affecting me as an adult. What right did I have complaining, I'd say to myself when other people had it so much worse. I had counseled individuals that had experienced such blatant traumas. The funny thing was that I could feel much of the same pain they were feeling, and these feelings went beyond simply my ability to empathize. This pain was there in spite of the fact that my childhood looked so much better than many of those I had counseled. Obviously, there was more pain in the family system than met the eye, and it affected me very deeply.

I came from a family that loved me, fed me, bought me more than adequate material things, and took me on trips. I had two parents that stayed married, went to church, and provided well. Yet, there were problems: I had a nauseated feeling in my stomach much of my childhood, cried a lot, and became overweight as a teenager. But, by owning my problems and looking at the causes resulting from my family system, I am now able to feel grateful for the positive aspects of my upbringing.

I have looked at many of the patterns and issues often over time, beginning with a family therapy class in my late 20s. That was the first time I could look and see everything was not perfect in my family of origin. I looked at the patterns between my parents and how they related. I looked at their parents and what they must have experienced. I learned a great deal. For one, there was poor communication and little ability to resolve conflict, disagree, show anger or depression, or problem-solve when there was disagreement. These unsuccessful patterns came from both of my parents' family systems.

Yes, I acknowledge, there were many positives that these two family systems gave me; such as, tremendous will power, the ability to develop as an individual, appreciation and love for myself as I am, and permission to think and question life. When we are healing, it is helpful to look at the challenging aspects of our past. I do not think this is disloyal to our parents, because their patterns of behavior were the product of their family systems also. No one is to blame. I encourage you to write your story. As you read this book, allow your memories to surface. Then write them down. It is healing to write.

Those of you who believe you can change patterns and heal the past will find this book of value. It will help you heal the places where the past has hurt you. Never will it allow you to focus blame on a person outside of yourself—mothers especially take a lot of blame in our society. The focus is on self-healing and taking personal responsibility for your own life. Just becoming aware of why you hurt and where you need help is not enough. In this book you will learn the tools to clear away the unwanted patterns and behaviors by learning to be who you really are, a shining essence of spirit in physical form. I want to help you find your True Self, which is much bigger than the family you were born into. You have the power to get back to basics and this simple book illustrates what you can do to change your life. You have the power to love yourself, beginning now.

Let us begin with the Acorn Analogy on the following page to show you that you are doing your best under the conditions in which you began.

Love,
Suzanne, 1995

NOTE: This book contains information from Suzanne's earlier books: *You Could Feel Good*, *Empowering Teens to Build Self-Esteem*, and the *Curriculum Guide for You Could Feel Good*.

Acorn Analogy

Deep inside,
you know how to be you;
just as an acorn knows how to be a mighty oak.

Remember, the acorn is doing the best it can do
at each stage of growth along its life cycle.
It can only grow to the degree that it has nurturing
from nature: sunlight, rain water,
and nutrients from the soil.

Even if the early start was less than optimal,
the eager oak can accelerate its desire to grow
at any time there are proper nutrients available.

YOU ARE LIKE AN ACORN!
You, too, are doing your best under
the conditions in which you are growing.
Add a little awareness, self-acceptance, and nurturing;
then watch yourself grow.

May this book nourish you to grow again
into your TRUE SELF, and help you
reclaim your birthright of feeling worthy.
You deserve to be who you are.

Part I

Getting Started

Learn to Love Yourself

It was a rude awakening for me to find that many of my problems stemmed from low self-esteem and not loving myself. I learned I was the only one responsible for loving me. No longer could I be the victim of other people's moods and low self-esteem. To this day, I must remember to put into practice all that I will teach you because my first response to others who are rude, angry, blaming, or emotionally destructive, is to feel rejected or wounded. I "catch" myself quickly now. This was not the case when I was new to the journey of self-healing.

To succeed in being who you are, you need these parts of you working together: your mind, your heart, and your power. This book will initiate all three.

Remember, if I can learn to put these ideas into practice and heal my feelings of inadequacy and unworthiness, so can you. It begins very simply with a decision right now to love yourself.

Here's how! Begin the process of loving yourself by taking the Harrill Self-Esteem Awareness Indicator. Here you will learn the areas where you need to concentrate.

The indicator is a tool to help you become more aware of yourself. It is not a test and is not to be used as a valid or concrete measurement of your self-worth.

The Harrill Self-Esteem Awareness Indicator

Rate yourself on a scale of 0 to 4 based upon your current feelings and behaviors:

0 = I never feel or behave that way.
1 = I rarely feel or behave that way.(25% of the time)
2 = I sometimes feel or behave that way.(50% of the time)
3 = I usually feel or behave that way.(75% of the time)
4 = I always feel or behave that way.(100% of the time)

Score   Self-Esteem Statements

_____1. I accept myself the way I am right now. I like being who I am.

_____2. I am worthy simply because I am alive. I do not have to earn my worthiness.

_____3. I get my needs met before I meet the needs of others (exception: young children).

_____4. I do not let it bother me when other people blame or criticize me.

_____5. I always tell myself the truth about what I am feeling.

_____6. I do not compare myself with other people.

_____7. I feel of equal value to other people regardless of my performance, looks, I.Q., achievements, or possessions (or lack of them).

_____8. I take responsibility for my feelings and emotions. I do not blame others when I am upset, angry, or hurt.

_____9. I learn from my mistakes rather than use them to confirm my unworthiness.

_____10. I separate my behavior from my inner-self, or spiritual essence.

_____11. I understand that I can choose to love each human being without having an active relationship with them.

_____12. I accept other people as they are, even when they do not meet my expectations or if I dislike their behaviors or beliefs.

_____13. I am not responsible for anyone else's actions, needs, thoughts, moods, or feelings, only for my own (exception: your children when they are young).

_____14. I feel my own feelings and think my own thoughts, even when those around me think or feel differently.

_____15. I am kind to myself and do not use "shoulds" and "oughts" to put myself down with value-judging comments.

_____16. I allow others to have their own interpretation and experience of me.

_____17. I look for something positive in each individual I meet.

_____18. I forgive myself and others for making mistakes and being unaware.

_____19. I accept responsibility for my interpretation of other people's behavior and my response to them.

_____20. I do not dominate others or allow others to dominate me.

_____21. I am my own authority. I make decisions that are in my own and others' best interests.

_____22. I develop and use my talents.

_____23. I balance giving and receiving in my life. I have good boundaries with others.

_____24. I am responsible for changing what I do not like in my life.

_____25. I choose to love and respect every human being, including myself.

Add up your score. There are a possible 100 points. Place no judgments on your score.

How to Use This Information

Your self-esteem indicator rating is important only to you and is not to be compared with anyone else's. Save the indicator and date it. Notice your high and low answers, but do not evaluate your worthiness based on your scores. Answer the questions again every few months, date your answers, and notice your scoring.

Low answers help you to become aware of beliefs and patterns that block you from feeling good and loving yourself. These answers illuminate the areas where you can help yourself by creating personal affirmations. Write your low-scoring statements on 3X5 cards. Read them out loud to yourself daily. Tape them in places you will see them often: refrigerator, bathroom mirror, your purse or wallet. You will see growth and improvement as you work on your lower areas, but do not judge the speed of your progress. Grow and expand your awareness at your own rate.

If many of your answers are low, you will notice quick improvement by applying the information in this book. All of the parts of you are interdependent, and a gain in one area strengthens your entire self. Take the Self-Esteem Indicator periodically to discover where you are growing and where you still need to work.

If you scored high, fine-tune your awareness by noticing your low areas—even if only one or two. Use this indicator to understand other people also.

Part II

What Is Self-Esteem?

What Is Self-Esteem?

Self-esteem is how you feel about yourself. You consciously and unconsciously send thoughts and opinions about yourself to yourself. These thoughts can be accurate and helpful or they can be false and damaging. To build self-esteem, you need to consciously think and say positive, honest things to yourself in your mind with your self-talk.

What is HIGH Self-Esteem?

High self-esteem is a feeling of total acceptance and love for yourself as you are. It is respecting and valuing yourself as a worthwhile human being. It is honestly seeing your good and not-so-good points. And, it is taking care of and nurturing yourself so you can become all you are capable of being.

High self-esteem is a quiet, comfortable place of enjoying and accepting who you are.

Myths About Self-Esteem

Myth #1: Self-esteem is earned. (False)

Truth: Self-esteem is your birthright and cannot be earned. It is a gift from the Source of your being to be accepted by you with no strings attached.

Myth #2: People with good looks, good jobs, and high I.Q.s have high self-esteem. (False)

Truth: Society praises certain traits which often are not all that healthy. What happens when a beautiful woman ages if she bases her self-esteem on her physical beauty? Is she any less worthy? NO! What happens when an athlete can no longer make millions of dollars because of physical injuries? Is he/she any less worthy? NO! High self-esteem is an inner experience. People who base their worthiness on their beauty or on achievements that others outside themselves applaud will suffer the minute they are not receiving others' acknowledgement. Do not assume good looks, jobs, or I.Q. automatically give one healthy self-esteem.

Myth #3: Having high self-esteem is being narcissistic. (False)

Truth: Developing high self-esteem is focusing on yourself for a while to get to know who you are, to heal and make peace with the past, and to open you to your potential. Narcissism is a diagnostic term used by mental health professionals to classify a person for treatment purposes. It is an infantile state where a person is stuck emotionally in the past and unable to think beyond self and relate to others. With high self-esteem, a person is responsive to others as well as self.

Myth #4: When you love yourself too much, you will take advantage of and hurt others. (False)

Truth: When you love and respect yourself, you automatically love and respect others and want to act responsibly. You grow into seeing everyone as an extension of yourself, auto-matically knowing when it is appropriate to put your needs before another's and vice versa.

Myth #5: It is bad to love and think highly of yourself. You will become obnoxious and brag about yourself. (False)

Truth: It is good to love and think highly of your-self. It allows you to grow into your poten-tial. A person who loves him/herself is better able to understand and forgive those who brag about themselves and push themselves and their ideas on others (both symptoms of low self-esteem).

Myth #6: If you love yourself too much, you will not be able to love others. (False)

Truth: You can only love others to the degree that you love yourself. You cannot give what you do not have.

Myth #7: High self-esteem comes from being appreciated and admired by others. (False)

Truth: High self-esteem comes from an internal validation of self—not from an external validation of self. Any time you depend on others to gain good feelings about yourself, those feelings evaporate when the others are not around, are having their own problems, or have low self-esteem. Do not turn your power to experience love over to others. Rather, turn inward and receive power from the Spiritual Source of your being.

Characteristics of High Self-Esteem

To empower yourself to build self-esteem, it is useful to know where you are headed. The following is a partial list of characteristics you will have when you have high self-esteem:

- Feeling worthy of love and respect.

- Liking yourself.

- Knowing yourself and only trying to be you.

- Being kind to yourself and others.

- Taking risks and learning new things.

- Accepting yourself even if you want some parts of you changed.

- Honestly assessing your strengths and weaknesses without excessive pride or shame.

- Taking responsibility for your own life. Admitting when you have a problem or make a mistake.

- Making amends if you find you have hurt someone.

- Developing your talents and interests.

- Balancing doing and being.

- Learning from your mistakes.

- Being willing to accept the consequences of your choices, with regard to your thoughts, feelings, and behaviors.

- Standing up for yourself, being assertive.

- Loving being you.

- Feeling a sense of social responsibility that goes beyond self.

- Feeling capable of living a productive life with meaning and purpose.

- Living life as a process of growth and change.

Add to this list by observing yourself and the people around you.

Reasons Why People Have Low Self-Esteem

A few of the more common reasons people develop low self-esteem are:

- Believing the negative and hurtful words and actions of others.

- Living with people who do not love and respect others.

- Having negative thoughts about performance, appearance, family, socio-economic level, and I.Q., among others.

- Being over- or under-protected as a child.

- NOT being taught, "I am good and of value and loved no matter what."

- Doubting that you were loved by one or both parents (the absence of a parent hurts, too).

- Being punished without ever being taught to separate "you" from your bad behavior.

- Living in fear.

- Being compared to others or to perfect standards that could not be met.

- Being raised in a dysfunctional family.

- Thinking "you" are your possessions, clothes, car, grades, job, or I.Q., rather than the inner self experiencing them.

- Not learning from your mistakes.

- Forgetting that you have a wise, intuitive, inner self.

- Forgetting that you are a spiritual being.

Recognizing People With Low Self-Esteem

How do you know if you or someone you know is suffering from low self-esteem? You receive clues by noticing extremes in people's behaviors, thinking patterns, and emotional responses. Following are characteristics of people with behaviors of low self-esteem, thoughts of low self-esteem, and feelings of low self-esteem. Add to these lists by observing yourself and the people around you.

Some BEHAVIORS of Low Self-Esteem

- Hurting yourself in any way.

- Being a bully or hurting others.

- Saying mean or abusive things to others.

- Not keeping your body, hair, or clothes clean.

- Not speaking up for yourself.

- Talking too much or too little.

- Needing to always be first or last.

- Gossiping or making fun of others.

- Breaking things or defacing property.

- Taking things that do not belong to you.

- Over- or under-eating.

- Not trying new things because you might make a mistake.

- Using alcohol or drugs to stop your pain, to hide your feelings, or to avoid solving problems.

Some THOUGHTS of Low Self-Esteem

- Thinking you are better than someone who differs from you.

- Thinking others are better than you.

- Thinking mean or negative things in your mind about yourself.

- Believing, "I don't count. My life does not matter."

- Thinking with "shoulds" or "oughts."

- Secretly hoping someone will fail or hurt him/herself.

- Thinking only one way—your way—is right.

- Forgetting to think about improving your life.

- Pretending everything is "okay," when it is not.

- Thinking you don't need anybody or any help.

- Thinking you can't make it without a partner (codependent).

- Blaming others when things do not go your way.

- Thinking prejudicial thoughts or scapegoating another person or group of people.

- Dominating others with your opinions or values.

- Being intolerant of individual differences.

- Not liking to look at your beliefs, values, and opinions in order to update them.

- Needing to be "right."

Some FEELINGS of Low Self-Esteem

- Feeling hatred, resentment, or a desire to get even.

- Feeling that you must be perfect to be okay.

- Feeling jealous and possessive.

- Feeling wounded or hurt when others with low self-esteem put you down.

- Often feeling angry or sad when you don't know why.

- Feeling embarrassed or shameful when you haven't done anything wrong.

- Crying a lot.

- Isolating yourself from others.

- Feeling lonely much of the time.

- Feeling too much dependency on another.

- Feeling a sense of failure and depression.

- Feeling unworthy of love and happiness.

- Feeling fearful of taking positive risks.

- Emotionally reacting to people and events instead of responding.*

- Fearing that you are not able to take care of yourself.

* An example of this might be that a person says something that hurts your feelings. That hurt is your emotional reaction. At this point, you can continue this emotional reaction by lashing out and saying something hurtful back. Or, you can take a deep breath and communicate in a calm but assertive manner that what they said was hurtful to you and not to say/do that again. This is a more empowered response.

What Keeps Low Self-Esteem Alive?

- Denying hurtful feelings, thoughts, beliefs, and perceptions about yourself.

- Believing it is shameful to get help and admit shortcomings.

- Saying negative things to yourself with the talk inside your mind (self-talk).

- Staying so busy that you do not have time to feel emotional pain.

- Expecting life or others to meet your emotional needs and not taking responsibility for your own life.

- Not updating the beliefs and values that were handed to you from childhood.

- Not working to understand your emotional triggers (reactions to people and events).

- Believing you are a victim of life and do not have any power to improve things.

- Being passive, being fear-ridden, and not taking positive risks.

- Not reading self-help books and/or not going to self-growth classes or therapy.

Part III

The Eight Keys to Loving Yourself

The Eight Keys to Loving Yourself

Now we are ready to look at some important concepts that can help you learn to love yourself. As you begin to think more positively, you will notice a shift in how you feel about yourself. Eventually your behavior will change to support the shifts in your thinking and feelings.

Following are eight important keys to help you think in a more positive, healthy way towards yourself. Some of you may already know these key concepts to loving yourself. If so, they are here to remind you of what you already know. Others of you may find these concepts new and different from what you have been taught. If they are a stretch for your mind, go slowly and ponder them for a while. Remember, the concepts and the perceptions you hold at present about life may not have taught you how to build your self-esteem and to love yourself. You are looking for information outside of your frame-of-reference to help you solve your problems.

The Eight Keys to Loving Yourself

The following concepts have changed my life:

1. Accept yourself as you are right now.

2. Look inside yourself, not outside yourself, to feel good.

3. Stop value-judging yourself.

4. Separate "YOU" from your behavior.

5. Stop comparing yourself to others or to a "perfect" standard.

6. Know you are doing your best.

7. Know you are worthy of unconditional love.

8. Take responsibility for your life.

1. Accept Yourself as You Are Right Now

Accept yourself right now just the way you are with no strings attached. The perfect time in the future with the perfect you does not exist.

You are okay just the way you are, even if you want to change parts of your self.

The Acorn Analogy helps us to see that the oak tree is perfect at each stage of its growing—as a seedling, as a sapling, and as a full grown tree.

You build your self-esteem and empower yourself by remembering that, like the oak, you are beauty and perfection at each place along your life path.

Affirmation:
It is always right now.
I love myself today!

More information:

Practice accepting yourself right now the way you are. It no longer serves you to wait until the future to love yourself. Have you ever heard anyone say, "I'll be happy when I get my degree" or "...when I lose weight"or "...when I am a parent"? Then when the person experiences what was supposed to make him/her feel happy, the happiness does not last. That perfect time in the future with the perfect you does not exist. The sooner you learn to accept yourself, now, as you are with no strings attached, the better you will feel. The paradox is that this attitude of acceptance is the ingredient required to create what you want in your future behaviors, attitudes, and goals.

Remember, your inner self is okay just the way you are, even if you want to change parts of yourself. Self improvement is easier when you accept who you are first.

2. Look Inside Yourself, Not Outside Yourself, to Feel Good

"Out there" is dependent upon other people or other things to make you feel good. "In here" (your thoughts, beliefs, attitudes, and perceptions) is the only thing over which you have complete control.

You must ultimately rely on yourself, not the opinions or actions of others, to feel good about yourself.

Affirmation:
I build my good feelings by looking within
and connecting with my True Self.

More information:

High self-esteem requires a person to have an internal locus of control as opposed to an external locus of control. This external validation of self was necessary as a child in order to fit into family and society. Most of us acquired our level of self-esteem from the approval of those outside of ourselves. As young teenagers, we paid a lot of attention to our peers, furthering our dependency on external validation of self. Many adults never grow beyond this external level of acceptance; and thus, the term was coined "keeping up with the Joneses." It is necessary to make the leap from external validation of self to internal validation of self to truly empower ourselves with high self esteem.

Practice looking inside yourself, not outside yourself, to feel good. Many of you have been taught to evaluate your self-worth by outer appearances and accomplishments—looks, educational degree, car, house, children, and other people's opinions of you. In reality, sound self-esteem must come from within you and not from the outer world. "Out there" is dependent on other people—the weather, economic cycles, family, jobs, and a host of other factors. These factors shift and change, and you will be affected by them if you evaluate who you are based on what happens to other people or events outside of yourself. "In here" (your thoughts, beliefs, attitudes, and perceptions) is the only thing over which you have complete control.

High self-esteem emphasizes the inner self that many of us have forgotten with our current lifestyles. There is nothing wrong with achieving. However, the motivation must be to fulfill and to please your inner self. Only when recognition and belief in yourself come from within are you able to accomplish or achieve with real satisfaction. When you achieve for other people's recognition and acceptance, you will not feel satisfied when others are not around to compliment or acknowledge you, and your good feelings about your accomplishments will not last.

There is nothing wrong with listening to what others say about you and accepting their feedback. In fact, sometimes this is useful. The important thing is that you must ultimately rely on yourself, and not on the opinions of other people, to feel good about yourself.

3. Stop Value-Judging Yourself

It is helpful to drop "shoulds" and "oughts" from your vocabulary. They are a form of value-judging yourself. It is irrelevant what you should do or should have done.

It is more important to ask yourself what you are or are not willing to do. Then do it or forget it.

Affirmation:
I am willing to pay the consequences of my
choices (both positive and negative);
this builds my self-esteem.

More information:

Practice stopping value-judging yourself and others. "Shoulds" and "oughts" are value-judgments. Judging yourself or another lowers self-esteem. When you say to another or when you think, "You should...," you really mean, "If I were you, I would..." Since no two people have exactly the same early environment, life experiences, genes, perceptions, and beliefs about life, it is unfair to expect others to do what you would do in their place. If you use "shoulds" and "oughts" with others, know that you are probably doing the same thing to yourself. When you use an "I should" message, you have self-talk telling you that you should feel guilty for not doing something, which is probably somebody else's value system or wish for you. If you do not have the will to carry out the "I should" message, it is important to spend time with yourself, a friend, or a counselor to see whether you really want to do the "I should" or not. It is important to get in touch with the consequences of your choices and to make sure they fit in with your value system.

It serves no purpose to beat yourself up mentally when you are unable to do what you wish you could do. Reminding yourself that you are working in that direction and that change is a continuing process can help. It is helpful to ask yourself, "Do I really want to do this?" or "Do I think I should do this to please another?" It is more relevant to ask yourself, "Will I or won't I do this?" and "Am I willing to pay the consequences of my choices?"

Some teachers and managers believe it is good to use "shoulds." A teacher once asked in a workshop, "If I don't put 'You should have...' on a student's paper, what do I write?" This is a very important question for people in positions of authority. Feedback is important, yet only emphasizing errors perpetuates low self-esteem in others. After finding a positive, you can say, "You could... the next time," or "It is helpful to...," or simply state the facts, such as "needs more detail," or "no main idea," or "illegible—neater handwriting required to pass." There does not need to be a value-judgment on the worth of the student when giving constructive feedback. If the student did poorly, that is information, not a reason to make him or her feel "inferior and unworthy."

4. Separate "You" From Your Behavior

You are not your behavior, but the one who behaves. You can dislike a behavior without disliking yourself.

If you have a behavior that you do not like in yourself, know there is a reason for this negative behavior. When you discover your hidden needs and intentions, you will improve your choices of behavior, because you will see what is motivating you.

Journal writing or talking to someone helps.

Affirmation:
I am getting to know my inner self so I can
wisely choose my behavior.

More information:

Practice separating "YOU" from your behavior and accomplishments. Your needs motivate you to behave in certain ways based on your guiding beliefs. Different people may get the same need met with different behaviors depending on the background, beliefs, values, and perceptions of each person. The more aware you are, the wiser your choices of behavior will be. Thinking affects your behavior, and you can think better if you are kind to yourself. Problem-solving is an important part of feeling good. You do this better when you are able to objectively look at your behavior aside from the okayness of your inner self.

If you have a behavior that you do not like in yourself, you raise your level of self-esteem by remembering that you are okay even if your behavior is not. If someone close to you behaves in a manner that is unacceptable to you, it is important to communicate that it is their behavior you do not like and that you always love them as a person.

5. Stop Comparing Yourself to Others or to a "Perfect" Standard

Your worthiness is innate. You lower your self-esteem if you feel "better than" or "less than" anyone else.

You have only to be you. Perfection is a goal, not a standard to measure your worthiness. Know you are learning and growing with all the experiences in your life.

If you must compare, do it only with yourself to gauge your progress and to set goals.

Affirmation:
I am incomparable. I am who I am.

More information:

Practice avoiding comparison and competition with others. Competition and comparison are part of most people's upbringing. Most of our schools, sports, jobs, and parenting styles are set up this way. There is a current belief that competition and comparison are healthy and necessary. However, the way we view competition tends to produce low self-esteem. When you compare yourself with someone else to get your good feelings, there will always be a winner and a loser. Life is not a race. We all live our life path in our own way and in our own time. Standards of excellence are necessary to gauge progress and mastery, but are not a measurement of our worthiness. Other people may still use competition incorrectly, but you do not have to buy into it.

Everyone has at least one gift and it will serve you to find out what yours is. It does not matter whether your gift makes you "Number One" in some widely appreciated activity, or just makes you quite good at something not generally appreciated. It can be an abstract gift such as being able to understand what other people (or animals) are feeling or communicating. It does not matter whether or not it has competitive value. To figure out what your gifts are, pay attention to what your interests are, and what you observe in others that you would like to experience.

6. Know You Are Doing Your Best

You can only do what you do based on your level of awareness. If you want to change, you must gather new information from teachers, self-help books, counselors, and observation of others to expand your choices.

There are many parts of you—physical, emotional, mental, and spiritual. If you are dissatisfied in one area, for example intellectual performance, it may help to work on the emotional part of you which, in turn, helps the mental. A positive change in any area helps all of you.

Forgive yourself for making mistakes and for taking time to change. I remember the Acorn Analogy to help me practice this idea.

Affirmation:
I nurture myself today
with awareness and good thoughts
so the acorn within me can grow.

More information:

Practice knowing that you are always doing your best. This is a difficult concept for many people to accept. Just for a moment, consider it a possibility. Remember that each person has a different level of awareness based on his/her early programming, perceptions, life experiences, beliefs, genes, etc. You can act only out of your present level of awareness to meet your current needs. If you are unaware of your needs, you may be surprised at some of your behavior. When you are unhappy with your behavior, even if you have been capable of acting the way you wanted to in the past, it is helpful to look at your needs. Your needs may be competing with each other and some of them may be unhealthy. When you become aware of your hidden needs, you will see the conflicts that keep you stuck doing things you do not like to do. Awareness gives us choices.

An example may be, "I want to be thinner, so I will limit my fat intake." The first couple of days I do okay, but then overeat rich food on the third day. Rather than shame and blame myself with critical mind talk, I can help myself make different choices if I look at the needs which motivate my behavior. I need to please myself by eating better to be thinner, but I find I have a deeper, stronger need to feel comfortable. When I am stressed, do not eat breakfast, or have an argument with my husband, I eat rich foods. I must learn how to

manage my stress, maybe by deep breathing, not skip-
ping meals, or writing my husband a letter to honor
my feelings and sort out my thoughts. As I do this, I
can make my need to be thinner the most dominant
need and can limit my fat intake as agreed upon within me.

7. Know You Are Worthy of Unconditional Love

Being worthy cannot be earned by your accomplishments or your behaviors. It is a gift to be accepted by you from you. You are worthy because you exist—it is your birthright.

Love yourself unconditionally—even if no one else knows how to do this for you.

_____

Affirmation:
I deserve love and respect, no matter what.
I remember to love myself unconditionally.

More information:

Practice unconditional loving. It is important to learn to love unconditionally in order to feel good about yourself. (Substitute the word "accept" if "love" is not comfortable.) Unconditional love is what the Greeks called agape love—love that has no reasons and no boundaries. It simply is love given without an expectation of a return. Conditional love, on the other hand, has to be earned, and there are expectations placed on either yourself or on the person to whom you are relating in order to be loved.

Examples of conditional love are: "I would love myself if I were thinner or if I had more money." "I love you as long as you meet my expectations and please me."

With unconditional love you are worthy simply because you are alive. There are no reasons for this love and acceptance. In the process of learning to love unconditionally, you need to see where you have placed expectations on your love, then you need to let go of them. It is an ingredient of sound self-esteem to love yourself unconditionally first; this will then allow you to love others unconditionally.

Unconditionally loving others does not mean you have to be around and tolerate abusive behavior. You can choose to love another or yourself, regardless of the behavior exhibited. Compassion and understanding help you forgive bad behavior so you can love unconditionally. Unconditionally loving yourself is important because we all go through the process of aging. Some of us have the challenge of being ill or are physically impaired. Stop over-identifying with your body and love the "You" that lives in your body.

Learn to practice unconditionally loving yourself, because other people in your life may not know how to unconditionally love you.

8. Take Responsibility for Your Life

No one is to blame for the problems you are experiencing—not you, not your parents, not your partner, not your children—no one.

Accepting responsibility begins the process of seeking a solution. Only you have the power to solve your problems and live your life more fully.

Change what can be changed, accept what cannot be changed. Only you have the inner power to do this.

Affirmation:
I take responsibility for my life now!

More information:

Practice taking responsibility for your life. No one is to blame for your unhappiness. This may be one of the most powerful points in this book and very difficult to put into practice. We all compile lists of grievances against others and against ourselves. Know that when you blame others, you are usually harder on yourself. Blame, shame, and guilt lower self-esteem and are demotivators in the process of change and growth. Many people begin their self-growth path by blaming their parents for "mistakes" in childrearing. It serves no purpose to blame your parents or anyone else. Remember that everyone is doing the best they are capable of doing with their level of awareness, and that includes your parents and their parents. Going beyond shame and guilt requires you to make peace with every person in your life who has ever upset, betrayed, or victimized you. You do this through love and forgiveness. Some of you may need to spend much time in counseling sessions and writing in your journal. Making peace with the past is an inner experience. Other people may or may not be a part of the healing.

Genuine forgiveness is not pretending you are mature, looking down upon the person who has wronged you, and letting them "off the hook." Instead, it is understanding how and why the other person could do what they did. You realize you forgive them because they really did not do anything to "you." They were merely acting out their life dramas with their own perceptions, which may have been distorted and unhealthy. You happened to be the one in their path when they used you as a target for their pain and suffering.

This is simple to explain intellectually and very difficult to practice. You may need to release a lot of anger and pain before getting to this place of forgiveness. For example, some people scream into a pillow or in the shower, and this releases some of the tension. Other people get their anger out by hitting a pillow or kicking a bag. Some people cry, others talk to a friend or to a counselor, and others write angry letters in a journal but do not send them. When you hold on to grudges and blame, it poisons your space. When you forgive, it frees you.

If these ideas are new to you or difficult to understand, you may need to ponder them before you can accept them. The insights they offer can change your guiding beliefs about yourself and about how life operates, greatly improving your emotional well-being. Remember that building sound self-esteem is a process of learning to love and accept yourself as you are. This emotional change is what empowerment is all about!

Part IV

Guiding Beliefs

Guiding Beliefs

Now, we will go further in understanding how our minds affect how we feel about ourselves. You have a set of assumptions about life, human behavior, relationships, and yourself. Call these assumptions guiding beliefs, or rules you live your life by. Many of these beliefs are unconscious to you, and you do not remember ever having learned them. Yet, these are the beliefs that guide your life.

Many of your guiding beliefs are not true, and yet, they are strongly influencing your life. When you become aware of your guiding beliefs, you can reduce and finally eliminate any of them that restrict you and make you feel bad. What you believe to be true is true for you, even if the belief is false. For example, you may believe that if you go outside in the winter with wet hair, you will catch a cold. This is true if you believe it, and there is a good chance you will catch a cold when you go outside with wet hair if you really, really believe it. Another person might have the opposite belief and would probably not get a cold by going outside in the winter with wet hair. In both cases, it would not matter what other people might say contrary to your position (that is unless you are about ready to change your guiding belief). You know that you are right because you have proven it to yourself. Remember that both positions are true for the persons believing them. The challenge is to discover and live greater truths.

If you are having a problem, such as not feeling worthy and not loving yourself, it is necessary to bring your guiding beliefs to your conscious awareness so you can change the ones that are not supporting you. These beliefs are creating your interpretation of the events in your life and your reality. Some beliefs may be false and may be unhealthy for you. After all, many of these guiding beliefs were accepted when you were two, three, four, or five years of age. Since the mind matures around the age of sixteen, you can see how immature many of your beliefs must be.

Many of you were not taught some positive beliefs that can improve your self-esteem, and many of you were taught some undesirable ones that are not true. Notice as you read this section which of the following ideas make you uncomfortable and which ones make you react. These areas in your belief system may give you clues as to why you have blocked your ability to love yourself. It is not important that you agree or disagree. Simply consider these ideas that may be influencing some of your beliefs. Some of the following examples may actually be some of your guiding beliefs. It is helpful to continually uncover your guiding beliefs to help you in the process of individuation, being autonomous, and in charge of your own life. In doing this, you will begin to free yourself from other people's belief systems, which prevents you from being who you are capable of being—uniquely yourself.

Things You May Have Been Taught That Are False

Let us read and discuss several things that many people were taught that are false.

1. You cannot get what you want in life.
2. Expectations always enable you to get what you want.
3. Get your wants met before your needs.
4. You are a victim.
5. You have to go to church to have a good relationship with God.
6. You will feel good when you have the "right" job, mate, car, etc.
7. Mistakes are bad.
8. It is better to give than to receive.
9. Everyone is equal and has equal opportunities in life.
10. A difficult childhood cripples you for life.

(List more of your own.)

Now let us look at these false beliefs in more detail.

1. You cannot get what you want in life. (False)

Many of you learned that you are not worthy and will never be good or perfect enough to receive what you need and want in life. Since you do not question this false teaching, you do not ask for what you want. You still believe that you do not deserve it. Yet, the opposite is true. Remember, you are worthy simply because you exist. You cannot earn your worthiness. You have to accept your worthiness. You can still let your needs and wants be known, even though you think you are not perfect and, therefore, not deserving. The truth is that you can have whatever you are willing and able to accept in life. What you are willing and able to accept is based on your attitudes and guiding beliefs about deserving. Therefore, if you have been taught that you cannot get what you want in life, begin a correction at the guiding-belief level that allows you to accept what you ask for. At the very least, consider the possibility of receiving what you want.

When I become conscious of something I want to experience, express, own, or become, I first let it be a possibility. I go through my process of why I can't have it or don't deserve it. Then I begin talking back to myself. I ask myself why I want this. Is it worth working or striving for? Can I see in my mind that I will enjoy it in the future? Is it possible I would be burdened by it?

Once I've determined I want something and would receive value from creating it, I begin talking to myself again. For example, when I went to graduate school, I heard people say, "Don't go into counseling, the field is flooded. It's so competitive. You can't get a decent job without a doctoral degree." But when I decided a counseling career was a possibility and I wanted it, I would say things to myself such as, "Even if there is a shortage of jobs, I may as well be one who finds one. If anyone can find a job with just a master's degree, I will." It is important to know yourself and what your needs are. Begin getting your needs met and then move towards creating what you want. Consider going deeper than material needs and wants.

2. Expectations always enable you to get what you want. (False)

Unrealistic expectations set you up for disappointment. This may sound like a contradiction with what was just said; however, realize that you can go to the opposite extreme and demand too much. Living from either extreme blocks you. There is a place of thinking in expanded consciousness where two opposites are both true: this is called a paradox. You must always ask for what you want; however, let go of the outcome so that you do not force a specific conclusion. For example, you may be working on prosperity consciousness and find that results do not manifest as you expected. There is a clue here that you are inwardly blocking yourself with your guiding beliefs again. You may secretly believe that you are unworthy and, therefore, undeserving. It is helpful to look at what is realistic at this time and make the adjustment. Ask for what you want and let it happen the way it will. Do not assume that you know the best way. It can be a mental trap to force a result before you have removed the blocks that prevent you from being able to achieve what you say you want.

Be honest with yourself regarding what the current reality is. Using our earlier example of creating prosperity in your life, do not assume you can charge whatever you want when the cash flow is not there. You may create the polar opposite of prosperity—going into debt. You must stop tricking yourself. You are in the process of creating prosperity consciousness. It is important to know the reality of the moment and the risk necessary to move into the future self you are creating.

Unrealistic expectations of others set you up for disappointments. You have no right to use your control over others. This is a misuse of power. An example is using guilt or punishment to force a particular response or action from another. When you allow others to live and create their own lives, you will find sometimes that what you expect and what the other person can or is willing to do does not always match up. Again, look at what is realistic.

When you find that you have expectations, and we all do, then communicate to the other person what you need and want. Ask, then let go of whether the other person can meet your expectations. Sometimes they can, and sometimes they cannot. It is helpful to question their needs and wants and listen to their expectations. The bottom line is that you must learn to accept the reality of the situation. Some things cannot be changed just by expecting the change. When you have needs and wants dependent on another, you are co-creating this reality. By co-creating, I mean sharing a joint creation. If I want to create something in my life that only involves me, like a more fit body or a new job, I call the shots and take full responsibility. However, when what I want involves another person, I must share the responsibility for creating, which requires taking the other person's reality (needs, wants, perceptions, or goals) into consideration.

3. Get your wants met before your needs. (False)

In our society there is heavy emphasis on material measures of happiness. Often you are trapped into achieving or trying to get some object when what you really want is to be nurtured emotionally or spiritually. Rather than a new dress or a new car or eating sweets, what you may need is attention. You may just need someone to care about you, to listen to you, and to enjoy you. Or you may need direction in life in order to feel a sense of purpose. Your needs must be met before you can feel good. The next time you are driven to eat when you are not hungry or buy something on impulse, stop and ask yourself what you really need.

4. You are a victim. (False)

If you have not learned you are powerful and are creating your life, then you may believe that things just happen to you. You may feel there is nothing you can do to change negative situations in your life. You are a victim. This is how much of the world thinks.

I encourage you to take an honest look at how you are reliving your childhood patterns. When you were little, you did not have the power that you do today as an adult. When you were dependent and helpless, you couldn't take care of yourself, or leave, or get help. You have grown up now and you can make choices to support yourself. If you know this and cannot put into practice what is healthy and right for you, then give yourself a gift. Get professional help.

5. You have to go to church to have a good relationship with God. (False)

Actually, this is one of many beliefs you may have learned from good-intentioned religious teachings, and it can be very scary to question religious beliefs. You may have experienced a period of guilt if you separated from early religious teachings in your life. The higher the degree of autonomy that your early upbringing encouraged, which gave you permission to question and explore, the lower the degree of guilt you will feel. You formed many of your beliefs and opinions about God by how you were treated by the authority figures in your life, mainly your parents.

It is of primary importance to develop a personal relationship with the Universe, the Source, or God, whatever term you prefer to use, on the journey to finding yourself. This needs to take place regardless of your beliefs about God or religion. To know that there is a power greater than yourself is mandatory if you are to feel good about yourself. This power exists all the time and does not depend upon a church or its dogma. Churches and their rules were designed to serve and lead people who needed or wanted help to their Source. If you feel you must be in a church or in a certain religion in order to experience this power, and if you are unfilled spiritually, then I urge you to explore, question, and experience other aspects of life. For example, explore different religions, learn to meditate, go on a retreat, spend time in nature, and spend time alone each day pondering life.

A relationship with God exists whether you are conscious of it or not. It exists twenty-four hours a day, inside or outside of a church or system of teaching about God. The goal is not to follow certain rules, but rather to develop a personal relationship with God.

6. You will feel good when you have the "right" job, mate, car, etc. (False)

You are in the perfect place, this moment, to learn your greatest lessons. Yes, you have the power to create a better job or find a more compatible partner; however, remember that right now is where you are. Life is a journey and we never get "THERE" because there is always a new place to grow to with new needs and new wants. We create tomorrow by what we focus on today. Since it is today, you must wake up and remind yourself you are okay just the way you are. You can continue the talk by saying things to yourself such as, "I will take care of myself today. I will remember to nurture myself, pay attention to my feelings, and take a positive risk to get my life going in a new direction." A job or partner or new car does not make you feel good for long because you still have to live with yourself. Your power is in today. Love yourself right now and you will feel good regardless of the circumstances. Prepare to create, at your own pace, a fantastic future self!

7. Mistakes are bad. (False)

You are in the school of life and are learning lessons daily that move you on course toward your life's purpose and goals. Mistakes happen because you do not know or understand something and are unable, at that moment, to do anything else. When you find that you are repeating a pattern and making the same mistake over and over, it is not that you are weak or bad, it simply means that you are unaware of something. The discomfort of the repeated experience will eventually give you the impetus to gather information, to try something different, and finally to become conscious of more parts of yourself.

Treating mistakes as opportunities to become more conscious is a more constructive place to live from than criticizing and blaming yourself. You can love yourself even as you make a mistake. Forgive yourself for not being aware of all aspects of a situation.

8. It is better to give than to receive. (False)

This spiritual teaching was for people who were takers and unable to give. Giving and receiving are flip sides of the same coin. Some of you need to learn to receive without feeling guilty.

True unconditional giving, with no strings attached, requires you to give from a place of being filled up emotionally—giving from the overflow. You can receive this nurturing from Spirit if not from another person. Some people are emotionally nurtured by nature or animals.

What would the world be like if everyone could only give? Remember to balance your giving and receiving, they are two parts of one whole.

9. Everyone is equal and has equal opportunities in life. (False)

The essence of each human being is equally precious. The Universe needs each and every person to make the greater whole complete. However, each person is different. You do not have the same genes, early environment, life experiences, or level of awareness as anyone else. Therefore, it would be impossible to have any two people equal. This has been interpreted as negative by some; however, it is simply a fact of life. You make life easier for yourself when you know and accept your capabilities, talents, strengths, weaknesses, and potentials. You also make life easier when you make wise and realistic choices and put yourself in situations that are fair and advantageous for you.

Look at your life and see if there are some areas that do not feel good and are putting you under stress. You may be acting under the false impression that every opportunity is good for you and that you should take all of them. On the other hand, if your life feels good and you do not wish to accept an opportunity to do something else, consider staying where you are as an acceptable choice.

10. A difficult childhood cripples you for life. (False)

Unwise parents and a negative childhood may cripple your life for a time; however, blaming parents, who were themselves the products of a painful childhood, helps no one. You can break out of early negative patterns; you do not have to remain handicapped forever. Limitations can force us to grow in compassion and understanding. Again, professional help may be needed.

Things You May Not Have Been Taught That Are True

1. You are worthy and deserving of love.

2. It is good to love yourself.

3. It is okay to make mistakes and not be perfect.

4. Feelings are good.

5. Use your talents.

6. All behavior makes sense.

7. People are your mirrors.

8. You create your own life, and you are responsible for yourself.

(List more of your own.)

Now let us look at these beliefs in more detail:

1. You are worthy and deserving of love.

You may have been taught that you are unworthy and that you have to earn your worthiness. Even some religious teachings reinforce this state of conditional love. If your home, community, or your church taught you that you do not count and that you are unlovable until proven lovable, this concept may be difficult for you to accept. Know that there are religions and people in the world today who teach the opposite. Remember you are innately good and worthy of love. To reach the realization within yourself that this is true, you may need to study and contemplate the teachings of other philosophies and religions. You may need to meet someone who loves you unconditionally—a friend, teacher, or counselor. Eventually you will feel from within that you are good simply because you are a part of the "All-That-Is," God. Simply because you exist, you are worthy and good.

2. It is good to love yourself.

You are not selfish and conceited if you love yourself. You deserve love simply because you exist. When you accept and love yourself, you have the inner resources and strength to handle everything that life presents to you. You come from a place of being grounded and being filled up rather than from a place of weakness, emptiness, and neediness. You are able to give to others instead of hoping and expecting others to fill you up with love. You can give only what you have. As you love yourself more and more, your close relationships are balanced in giving and receiving.

3. It is okay to make mistakes and not be perfect.

If you were perfect, you would not need to be here. This is the school of life. When you correct your mistakes, you learn. I like the definition of perfection given by Ken Carey in VISION. According to Carey, "Perfection is not never making a mistake; perfection is never consciously making a mistake." So work towards the goal of mastery or perfection, learning along the way to live from your highest intentions and values.

4. Feelings are good.

Emotions such as anger and depression are not wrong or bad, they simply are. You can use anger, jealousy, or depression to feel bad or you can see them as feedback from within that something is not right and needs to be healed. Use feelings to help you understand your problems, use emotional energy to make changes in your life. Anger, for example, is considered a secondary emotion. The feelings behind anger are the primary problem. These feelings could include fear, insecurity, loss of control, or fear of abandonment. Learn to always tell yourself the truth about what you are feeling. Your inner guidance system wants to take care of you. Listen.

5. Use your talents.

Developing, enjoying, and sharing your talents makes you feel good about yourself. I'm using the word "talent" loosely; for example, it can mean the ability to listen to others or to work with animals or to care for plants. It feels good to share your talents. If the people now in your life do not accept or need what you have to give, there are many others who do. Volunteering is a way to practice your gifts and talents and is really not work at all, because you receive as much as you give. Think about what you love to do, then practice the skills by volunteering. At some point, you might choose to develop your talents into a job where you get paid for what you love to do.

6. All behaviors make sense.

If you do not like your behavior or another's, you can look behind the actions to see what is motivating you or the other person to act. Your needs motivate you. When you are surprised or disappointed at your own behavior, remember that you have competing needs. You may be unaware of some need you have brushed aside for a long time. As you become conscious of suppressed needs that are demanding expression, you will find ways to meet your needs instead of blaming yourself when they erupt in unwanted behavior. The more aware you are of your real needs, the easier it is to understand and to change your unwanted behaviors. Begin by seeking insight into your needs, not focusing on your behaviors. Journal writing helps. All behavior makes sense when we find out what needs are motivating ourselves and others. When we identify the needs, we have choices about how to get those needs met so we aren't surprised by negative behavior. Again, it is necessary to see your behavior as separate from the essence of you, the person.

7. People are your mirrors.

If you do not like another person's behavior, it is because you do not like a part of yourself. An example of this mirror concept is the psychological defense mechanism (where we defend ourselves from ourselves) called projection. We want to be "good," so we disown anything that does not fit into our image of good and project it onto someone else whom we then label "bad." This means we have made the judgment that a certain behavior or feeling or attitude is bad—so bad that it could not be a part of us—and we deny and suppress that part of ourselves to avoid facing and dealing with it as our own. When we do this, we are missing an opportunity to grow and to become more conscious of ourselves. We all have disowned parts of ourselves; the psychologist Carl Jung called these parts "the Shadow."

When I do not like someone's behavior, I ask myself many questions to see what I can learn about myself. What lesson do I need to learn from this situation? Who does this person remind me of in the past? What am I expecting or demanding from him/her? Why do I care? Am I hiding that same behavior from myself? Am I unconsciously doing it somewhere in my life? How does this fit into any of my patterns? What do I need that I am not getting that this person is now bringing to my conscious awareness?

This also works in a positive direction. When you like another person, it is because that person reflects something you like in yourself, or something you want to develop in yourself. You do not see anything in another person unless it is a part of yourself—a potential in you. Traits, feelings, and behaviors that do not match up with another simply go unnoticed and there is no response from you. As you learn to accept yourself, you will grow to accept all people regardless of their behavior. This does not imply that you have to be around those people you do not like. Just learn from them and work on yourself, not them.

I believe that in the process of change and growth, it is very important to "spend time" with people who reflect love, acceptance, support, interest, and caring. This can come from a friend, a therapist, or a support group. I have found that joining a support group is the way many people get the strength and courage to go forward. This is especially so when there is no support and encouragement to draw from in their daily lives.

8. You create your own life, and you are responsible for yourself.

Most of you were not taught that when you focus your thoughts, you put energy into creating those thoughts. The stronger your thoughts and images feel, the more powerful your creations are. They can be negative or positive. What you fear, you create as a goal because you spend so much time thinking about it. The good news is that if you do not like what you have created, you can change it. There is an unwritten law that requires you to use this power only for yourself. It is not to be used to create for other people—no matter how good your intentions are. However, you can align yourself with what another person is creating and add your power to what he/she wants to create. In other words, each person is responsible for his/her own life. It is actually possible to delay another person's growth by attempting to fix or change him/her or to take away his/her pain. The best way to help another is to work on yourself because you have an effect on those around you.

It is time to take responsibility for creating your own life, to live your own purpose and fulfill your own needs. When you do this, you build your self-esteem.

One simplified way of looking at your life is to see it in three stages. The first stage involves your parents and your life experiences from birth to around age eighteen. The circumstances of these years set up a matrix of patterns which you will work out in stage two. Self-awareness and wisdom are acquired in stage two. In this stage, you heal your conflicts and solve your problems. Some of you are experiencing issues of conflict that have been handed down from generation to generation in areas such as parenting, self-esteem, religion, alcoholism, chronic depression, communication in relationships, love, etc. Many people never move beyond stage two; they simply pass their patterns on to their children. This book is designed to help you work through stage two of your life. Stage three is reached when you truly know, love, and accept yourself as you are. Difficult early experiences need not prevent you from reaching stage three in your life. When you look at making peace with your childhood and resolving your conflicts, you see your parents and your early experiences as opportunities for growth.

One way to overcome the impact of early trauma is to go back over the memories in your mind, in as much detail as possible. You do this as an adult, having more mature insights into what was really going on. In this way you interpret your past and, thus, change its influence.

It is helpful to continue looking at your guiding beliefs to uncover those that no longer serve you. Thus, you will begin the process of becoming autonomous and being in charge of your own life. In this way, you will begin to free yourself from other people's belief systems which prevent you from being who you are capable of being—uniquely yourself.

Creating New Guiding Beliefs

Now, it is time to specifically work on your guiding beliefs which need to be updated. Get some paper and a pen. As you read this section, write down your beliefs as you become aware of them. Then create new beliefs by updating old, unhealthy guiding beliefs with new healthier ones. These new beliefs become affirmations to say over and over to yourself. Over time, you will live them.

Many people have a basic guiding belief that says, "I am unworthy." You can take this guiding belief and turn it into healing affirmations such as:

I am worthy because I am alive; I do not have to earn my worthiness.

I care about myself.

I accept myself, regardless of what other people think or feel about me.

I feel loving toward myself.

Following are many examples of limiting beliefs and corrected beliefs. Use this list to write some of your own. Put your updated beliefs on 3 x 5 cards and say them out loud to yourselves often. You may use my examples of positive guiding beliefs and/or you may create your own. The more individual and specific these beliefs are, the more powerful they will be for you.

Examples of Limiting Beliefs and Corrected Beliefs

Limiting = L   Corrected = C

Beliefs About Security:

L : I feel insecure when another person disagrees with me.

C: I am a worthwhile person regardless of whether or not we agree. My security comes from within, not approval by others.

Beliefs About Money:

L : To make money, I must give up free time.

C: I make money and I still have free time.

L : I am not willing to work long hours; therefore, I cannot have much money.

C: I make money, by using my time in creative ways. I have fun making money.

L: I am spiritually oriented; therefore, I cannot make a lot of money.
C: Money is not a sign of being spiritual or unspiritual. I have money and am spiritual at the same time.

L: People with a lot of money are selfish.
C: I can create money by just being myself.

Beliefs About Time:

L: I do not have time to do what I want.
C: I make choices with my time so that I include doing things that please me.

L: I am always late.
C: I am learning to be on time and I plan to be early for appointments.

Beliefs About Perfection:

L: I have to be perfect.
C: I am perfect right now just the way I am, even as I grow and change.

L: If I do not come in first, I am inferior and feel humiliated.
C: I am a perfect expression of myself, whether I come in first or not.

L : No one really likes me because I am "out of step" with others.

C : My special qualities attract the right people to me, and I release expecting everyone to like me.

L : No one will really love me because I am different from others.

C : My special qualities attract the love to me that I need. I like being different.

Beliefs About My Body:

L : No mate will really love me because I am no longer slender nor young enough.

C : I love myself just the way I am, in body, weight, age, and life experience. I let go of society's unhealthy images for me.

Beliefs About Men:

L : Men are run by their egos and hormones.

C : Men are perfect right now just the way they are. I find the men who are thoughtful and caring.

L : Men are inferior to women.

C : Men and women are different; each are human beings on life's journey.

Beliefs About Women:

L: Women are airheads, emotional, and unable to work hard.

C: Women can be creative and emotional, as well as logical and hardworking.

L: Only women know how to take care of young children because they are naturally nurturing.

C: Men can be nurturing and take good care of young children if they so choose.

L: Women are inferior to men.

C: Women and men both have good qualities. Gender does not determine worthiness.

Beliefs About Criticism:

L: I feel angry and threatened when I am criticized.

C: When people criticize me, they are doing their best to offer an opinion. I let go of having to believe every opinion I hear.

L: I feel bad and shameful when people criticize me.

C: I am good regardless of whether others find my traits and behaviors positive or negative.

Beliefs About Work:

L: I never can catch up with my work at my job.

C: I do my job perfectly in the time allotted me. I continually learn time management techniques to improve my efficiency.

L: Work is more important than play.
C: I balance work and play because they are both very important.

Beliefs About Agreement:

L: I feel insecure when others disagree with me.
C: I stop letting others' agreement with me determine my worthiness.

L: I feel unworthy when others disagree with me.
C: I am worthy and do not need others' agreement to feel good.

Beliefs About Being Right:

L: To feel safe, I have to be right, and not get into confrontations with others.
C: I let go of being right. I listen to others' opinions. We can disagree. I feel safe when others disagree with me.

L: I spend a lot of time proving I am right rather than being right.

C: I choose inner peace and let go of proving I am right.

Beliefs About Rejection:

L: My fear of rejection determines what I say and do.

C: I say and do what is right for me. If you reject me, that is your choice.

L: I feel insecure when you are emotionally distant.

C: I am strong within, and accept your emotional distancing when you are upset and in pain.

Beliefs About Wants:

L: I can only have what I need and not what I want.

C: I have what I need, so I can create what I want.

L: I am selfish if I want more.

C: I create from what I am, which is neither selfish or unselfish.

Beliefs About Value:

L: What I say is not important.

C: I express my opinions and thoughts because I am as important as everyone else.

L : I am not important.
C: My life makes a difference.

Beliefs About Selfishness:

L : I am uncaring and selfish if I put my needs first.
C: I am a caring, responsive, and giving person. Sometimes I choose to put myself first.

L : I don't have enough time for me.
C: I am learning how to identify my needs and nurture myself.

Beliefs About Public Self:

L : I can't speak before groups. I'm shy.
C: I can speak to groups because I have much to say. It does not matter if I am shy.

Beliefs About Self Love:

L : No one really cares for me. I'm unlovable.
C: I release myself from others' projections. I'm lovable and receive unconditional love from my Higher Power.

Beliefs About Codependency:

L : I must control what you do and solve your problems for me to feel safe.

C: I release needing to be needed and allow you to solve your own problems.

Beliefs About Partners:

L: I will be happy when the prince (princess) rescues me; then I will have found the perfect partner.

C: I am happy today learning to be exactly my true Self. I look within to feel happy.

Beliefs About Parenting:

L: I am a good mother/father when my children get good grades and have high achievements. If they don't, I have failed as a parent.

C: I am a good mother/father regardless of my children's grades and achievements. I care about my children. I encourage and communicate with my children daily. I do not get my self-esteem from my children.

Beliefs About Forgiveness:

L: I could never forgive my parents for hurting me when I was young.

C: I ask my Higher Self (Higher Power) to help me forgive my parents, who were unaware and were also victims of abuse.

L : I will never forgive you for what you have done.

C: I forgive you so I can release my emotional bondage to you. I free myself so I can heal.

Part V

Ways to Make Positive Changes

Ways to Make Positive Changes

This section of the book gives you practical things you can do to support your growth and inner healing. Just knowing what you should do and why you are the way you are doesn't necessarily ensure positive changes in how you feel or behave. Change starts with awareness, and you also need ways to anchor the new information within you.

Ways to empower you to put into practice the information in this book include the following:

- Write in a journal.

- Create a support system.

- Use creative visualization.

- Change your self-talk.

- Say positive affirmations.

Journal Writing

Journal writing is a unique way to get in touch with who you are, your thoughts, and your feelings. By writing what is inside you, inner healing takes place. Eventually you start remembering people and events that wounded you. This process allows negative memories and feelings to surface as these have been buried and are unconsciously affecting your life. As you write your reactions to people and events, you are recording your patterns, thoughts, and feelings. You can even use your journal to write letters to those you feel angry towards. Use your journal to list your needs, wants, wishes, hopes, and dreams. In this way, you begin transforming your life.

Try it for a month before you judge this method of self-healing. No one will check your grammar or spelling. This is only for you. Motivate yourself by using different colored ink pens, even calligraphy pens. Hide your journal where you know it will be safe. If you write something and you fear it will be read, send it to a friend for safe keeping or even rip it up once you've expressed yourself.

Write for about twenty or thirty minutes. Aim for five times a week. It helps if it is at the same time of day; but, by all means, write even if you are not a schedule person.

Following is a list of topics to get you started:

- Write a list of your needs, wants, desires, goals, and values.

- Record your dreams. Include how you feel about each dream and what you think it may mean. Look for themes and patterns in your dreams over a period of time.

- Write what you want to create and experience in life.

- List your blocks—the things that seem to keep you from a sense of happiness and well-being.

- List your fears.

- Write letters to anyone you feel angry or unforgiving toward. You do not have to mail the letters. In fact, it might be unwise to mail such a letter if you are feeling insecure or fearful. Wait until you have gained some self-confidence, and then decide whether or not to mail it.

- Answer the questions titled "Getting to Know Myself" on page 100 in *You Could Feel Good*.

- Write a poem of forgiveness to someone in your life. An example of a poem is on page 100 in *You Could Feel Good.*

- What is the difference between my "self" and my "Self"? How do you know which is speaking to you? (Hint: Look at the difference between the conditioned personality of your inner child from growing up in your family, school system, and society, and then look at yourself as an adult—the wise, intuitive, and spiritually-oriented "Self.")

- Who were the people and what situations influenced your self-esteem in your early life? as a teen? as an adult? Write about both your positive and negative past experiences.

- How do your past experiences affect you now?

- Answer for yourself: Who am I? Why am I here? What gives my life value and meaning?

- What changes in self-improvement are you working on right now?

- Name one change you want to complete after reading this book.

- How will these changes affect others around you? How will you handle this?

- What is the difference between conditional love and unconditional love? What did you learn about love in your family of origin? from your religious teachings? from the media?

- Write yourself a letter at the beginning of each year or on your birthday, expressing all that you want to experience and accomplish in the next year. Open your letter the following year and see how well you stayed on track. Notice whether you had expectations encompassing several months or several years. Then write your next year's letter with more realistic time frames.

Create a Support System

It is difficult to transform alone. Whether you realize it or not, having one other person to listen to you without judgment is very helpful in healing.

Some of you will benefit from counseling, while others will benefit from joining a group, such as a Twelve Step group, church group, or study group. Having others to call upon when you lose your courage to make positive changes is one of the best gifts you can give yourself. You open yourself to emotional support when you open to others and allow your vulnerability to surface.

A good way to start is by taking a self-awareness class; these are often offered in continuing education programs. You might even like to start a self-esteem study group yourself.

Creative Visualizations

Use creative visualizations to create what you want in life. Use them for creating all positive changes, from confidence and inner peace, to finding a job or life partner.

Visualizations are pictures that you see in your mind. Some people see clear visual pictures when they close their eyes and some do not. Some people are inclined to be more auditory (sense through hearing), and others are more kinesthetic (sense in terms of feeling).

Those of you who are not visual can still visualize by closing your eyes and sensing what you are creating in your mind. Practice a minute. Close your eyes and sense the difference between your car and your neighbor's car or between an apple and a pear. Your impression is visualization, whether you see the cars or fruit clearly or not.

Consciously working with visualizations is similar

to working with affirmations. You are creating your future by the conscious images you see in your mind today. Why not become aware of them and have them create positive realities for you!

If, for example, you want to feel confident giving a presentation at work, picture in your mind yourself breathing deeply, smiling, and feeling relaxed as you stand in front of your boss. The more you can feel the mind picture, the more it helps you create the picture in real life. You build your good feelings by seeing and feeling positive mind pictures.

You can take each of the affirmations presented in the next few pages and use them for visualizations. While you say one of the affirmations, close your eyes and imagine what it would look like and feel like if it were already true. This is a part of a lifestyle change. You make your affirmations more powerful by putting your mind behind your words in order to create what you want. You can use the visual technique to create anything you want to experience in your future. You can use it to break out of old patterns, to change how you relate to other people, to attract a relationship, or to build your self-confidence.

Change Your Self-Talk

To build good feelings about yourself, it is important to become your own best friend by saying kind, loving, supportive, problem-solving things to yourself. Start by identifying and healing negative self-talk.

You have a voice inside your mind that comments continually about everything you think, do, and say. This voice is critical and negative much of the time. To build self-esteem, it is necessary to change the negative, critical self-talk to a kind, loving, and supportive voice inside your mind.

Exercise:

Begin by remembering the past week. What negative feeling memories do you have? Choose one. Go back in your mind and remember the things you said to yourself in your mind. For example, perhaps you were impatient with your children and yelled and screamed at them, and your self-talk said, "You dummy, you didn't do it right, AGAIN! You are a bad mother. You'll never get it right. You are so stupid. I hate you for dumping your emotional garbage on your kids."

This negative self-talk lowers your self-esteem. To break out of repeating a negative habit such as yelling at your children, you need to break the cycle of inner abuse. Instead of beating yourself up in your mind, it is much more productive to build yourself up by saying kind, supportive, and problem-solving things to yourself.

A better way to talk to yourself would be, "I am working to change my behavior. I am doing better than

I was last year. I love my children and I will talk to them and express why I got so upset. I will journal-write about my feelings."

Listen to your self-talk. Talk back to it and you begin to feel better about yourself.

Affirmations

A most powerful tool for healing negative self-talk and negative guiding beliefs is to say affirmations. Affirmations are good things to say to yourself. Positive affirmations build positive self-talk which, over time, empowers you.

On the following pages are positive affirmations that build self-esteem. If you say the statements over and over, even out loud to yourself, you create positive self-talk in your mind, which eventually empowers you to feel good about yourself. After each affirmation is information to explain what the affirmation means.

Remember!

Say the statements over and over, out loud, until you feel like the affirmation is true about YOU. You might even like to read the affirmations into a tape recorder and listen to your tape while you are relaxing or going to sleep at night. Affirmations are also available from this author on a tape, *Affirm Your Self*, and on **Self-Esteem Cards**. See the order form at the back of the book.

Affirmations begin on the next page.

Let's get started!

I unconditionally love myself and others.

Expect no one to unconditionally love you. You must learn to do it for yourself by connecting to the spiritual essence within you.

I am my own authority.

When you are willing to pay the consequences of your choices, both positive and negative, you become responsible for yourself. Notice that you pay the consequences anyway, so why turn your power over to another?

*I am accepting of myself
when I make mistakes.*

 It is okay to make mistakes. All humans do. That is how people learn and grow. Forgiveness is important in order to get past the critical self-talk.

I stop comparing myself to others.

 Comparison lowers self-esteem. It creates a feeling of "less than" or "better than." You are neither. You are incomparable.

I connect with my inner self to feel good.

 Sound self-esteem is not based upon your outer appearances. It is a conscious expression on the outside of who you are on the inside. Get to know your inner spiritual Self.

I set appropriate boundaries for myself.

 It is okay to say "NO." Some experiences are not healthy for you.

I am responsible for my own life.

No one else is to blame or to be given credit for who and what you are. You have the power to create your life the way you want it to be. Awareness and risk-taking are the keys.

I allow people and events to "trigger" me in order to make peace with the past and become more aware.

Emotional reactions are bigger than the person or event triggering you. A reactive pattern of behavior results from many similar hurtful issues from the past. Examining emotional reactions allows you to be in the now, free of the past, and responsive rather than reactive.

*I give out of a sense of love
to the degree that I am filled up.*

It is important to get your needs met.
When you do, you have more to give
and without an expectation of a return.

I give up being an emotional victim.

You have a part to play when you
feel hurt. As you let go of
unrealistic expectations and accept
what cannot be changed, you will
no longer "set yourself up." Work
on yourself. As you change, others
will change in your presence.

I choose to develop and use my talents.

You build self-esteem when you express your gifts—whether playing the piano, writing, taking care of plants or animals, or listening to others. Talents do not have to be achievements valued highly in society.

I align myself with the higher will and purpose.

You have a special purpose only you can fulfill. This will be revealed to you as you grow spiritually. Begin with getting to know and accept your Self.

I am healing the pain and fear from my past.

A difficult childhood does not have to cripple you for life. You can heal your wounded inner child by loving and nurturing yourself. Understanding yourself and taking risks empowers you to break free of negative patterns. Remember, you are much more than your conditioned past.

I stop value-judging myself and others.

Value-judging is using "shoulds" and "oughts." It is irrelevant what you should do or should have done. It is more important to ask yourself what you are or are not willing to do.

I accept and allow myself to feel.

Feelings are not right or wrong. They simply are. They give feedback on what is going on within you. You can learn to put your feelings into words. Eventually, you can evaluate the thoughts behind the feelings. Changing your thoughts and beliefs can change how you feel.

I listen to the wisdom of my intuition.

My intuition guides and protects me. As I learn to hear this quiet voice within, I allow the spiritual wisdom to direct my life. This inner guidance from Spirit gives me the courage to move forward day by day.

I am doing my best at each moment
with my present level of awareness.

Your best includes looking at all aspects of yourself—physical, emotional, mental, spiritual. Go easy on yourself when you make a mistake, stumble and fall, or can not maintain or repeat a behavior or level of achievement.

I separate my behavior from the inner me.

You are a spiritual being. You are innately worthy even if your behavior is bad. Love and forgive yourself even when you do not like your actions, thoughts, or feelings. This builds sound self-esteem and helps you change unwanted behavior.

I make sense out of all my behavior.

You can understand all your behavior when you look for what conscious and unconscious needs you are trying to meet. Also look at your feelings and guiding beliefs to see what is behind unwanted actions.

I get my needs met with healthy choices of behavior.

If you want to change behavior—
• Listen to your thoughts and feelings.
• Determine your needs.
• Choose healthy ways to get those needs met.
• Take risks with new choices.

I expand my awareness and understanding of myself so that I will have greater free will.

You will make wiser choices when you know your inner needs, wishes, values, goals, guiding beliefs, and purpose.

I set realistic goals and expectations for myself.

Goals and expectations need to be constantly evaluated, adjusted, and prioritized. Standards set too low or too high lower your good feelings.

I cease blaming myself for undesirable actions, thoughts, and feelings.

 Take responsibility, not blame, for your choices. Blaming yourself lowers your self-esteem. Negative consequences teach you to make more aware choices in the future.

I see aspects of myself in other people. They are my mirrors.

 We all are capable of good and bad actions, thoughts, and feelings. Learn from everyone you meet instead of judging them. You can only see in others what is a potential within you. Emulate the people who reflect your goodness, love, beauty, and truth.

*I communicate with an intention
of being authentic and genuine.*

 Others may perceive even your good
intentions as negative. You and your
Higher Power know the truth of
your intentions.

*I let go of expecting everyone to like
and support me.*

 Some people may never like you,
especially when you begin being
who you really are, your True Self.

I accept myself right now the way I am.

This builds unconditional love, which allows you to grow and discover more and more of who and what you are. Your place of power is right now, today, to accept yourself.

I accept everyone wherever they are in their level of awareness.

Acceptance does not mean you have to be around someone who hurts you because they are unaware or wounded or fearful. It simply means understanding them with compassion.

I nourish myself with love and light from my Higher Self.

The energy from Spirit is the real source of your love, strength, and power. You are a multi-dimensional being—physical, emotional, mental, and spiritual.

I am worthy because I am alive.

You need do nothing to earn your worthiness. It cannot be earned. It is your birthright.

Now that you've read all the way through the affirmations, go back and choose one that does not feel true for you. Repeat the affirmation often until you really feel inside that it is true for you. Write it down and listen to what your negative self-talk says. Talk back to the self-talk until the affirmation goes into your consciousness.

Do this with any affirmation you do not have in your consciousness until all the affirmations feel true for you. Go at your own speed. If it does not feel "right" to work on a certain affirmation at this time, honor the resistance. Wait until your intuition guides you to work on it.

Part VI

Tying It All Together

Summary of Ways to Build Self-Esteem

Simple thoughts to remember:

- Only you can be you!

- You are responsible for your life, your choices (or lack of them), your interpretations of people and events.

- You pay the consequences of your thoughts, feelings, and actions.

- You are not your behavior.

- All behavior makes sense when you look behind the behavior to what needs are motivating you. Remember, you are like the acorn doing your best under the conditions in which you are growing.

- Honor your resistances and listen to your intuition.

Make the Eight Keys of Self-Esteem part of your beliefs about yourself.

Change guiding beliefs that are limiting, negative, and false.

If you believe you must earn love and worthiness from sources outside yourself, you may benefit from saying these two affirmations often:

- I am worthy simply because I am alive.

- I receive unconditional love from myself and do not expect this from others.

Keep a journal.

- Write your thoughts, feelings, and reactions to people and events.

- Write letters to people with whom you are angry, but do not give the letters to them.

Create a support system.

- Join a support group.

- Take classes.

- Team with a friend who is also working on self-discovery so you can share and encourage each other.

- There is power in numbers, so have people around you who know and live these concepts.

- Start a self-esteem study group. There is a self-esteem curriculum by this author to go with her book, **You Could Feel Good.** See the order form at the end of this book.

- Contact the National Council for Self-Esteem for the chapter in your area.

The National Council for Self-Esteem
PO Box 277877
Sacramento, CA 95827-7877
1 (800) 488-6273

Say kind things to yourself.

Change negative self-talk to positive self-talk by saying positive affirmations such as:

- I am okay even when I make a mistake.

- I love and accept myself even if my mother, father, friend, or teacher does not show love and acceptance of me.

- I am good even when my behavior is bad.

Visualize what you want in your mind.

Change negative self-images to positive pictures, such as:

- See yourself standing tall, taking a deep breath as you preview in your mind a positive way to handle a challenging situation you must go through.

- See yourself changing a negative habit to a healthy new behavior.

Develop and share your talents.

- Get involved and help others.

- Pass on what you've learned.

Symptoms of High Self-Esteem

- Accepting yourself and others.

- Feeling joyful and loving.

- Allowing yourself to make mistakes, stumble and fall, and occasionally fail.

- Taking positive risks.

- Feeling capable of solving your problems.

- Losing fearful thoughts.

- Living in the NOW.

- Losing interest in value-judging and blaming (no "shoulds" and "oughts").

- Smiling frequently.

- Allowing people and circumstances to unfold.

- Accepting what must be by recognizing what you cannot change.

- Being balanced physically, emotionally, mentally, and spiritually.

Part VI

Epilogue

Epilogue

Spirituality

This book teaches you how to empower yourself, giving many ideas and techniques to heal low self-esteem. Now, I will emphasize the importance of the spiritual aspect of healing self-esteem issues. We can do all the "right" techniques, correct our guiding beliefs and self-talk, journal write, heal our inner child of the past, and still have an empty feeling. We must at some point develop a personal relationship with the Source of our being to truly heal our self-esteem problems. What you call the Higher Power is not important. What is important is that you allow a personal relationship to develop with this spiritual power and surrender to its gift of Unconditional Love.

Remember that you are worthy of unconditional love; it is your birthright. Receive it from your Higher Power, your Higher Self, your Soul, God, the Source of your being. It matters not whether you build this relationship while in nature, meditating, communing with angels, or going to a church or temple. What matters is the direct experience of healing that comes from allowing this spiritual power into your life.

When disconnected from Spirit, it feels as if there are two parts of ourselves. One is the part of us living our day-to-day life on Earth with the little self, ego, or personality, struggling to find our way. The other is the spiritual part of us that is hard to grasp, touch, or experience with our five senses. Call this the Higher Self, Soul, or Transpersonal Self. We may know this spiritual part is there, but not have a direct experience of it. Instead, we get caught in the pain of our conditioned personality and feel like a child, needing something, but we do not know what. Our inner child, who may have experienced pain and suffering, dominates our reality and we feel a split from our Spirit. In reality, there is no split; the paradox is that we are one. Until we remember and are able to experience this oneness, it seems as if there is a separation or split within us, keeping us separate from others.

Many times this split shows up in relationship insecurities as we look for the perfect partner to make us feel safe and whole. Many people get sidetracked into falsely believing that romantic love, sex, money, or power are what they are looking for, wanting desperately to heal this split or void.

The truth is that you are capable and worthy of experiencing this wholeness, of moving from the powerless state of consciousness of the little self to an empowered Spiritually Awakened Being. The little self is created from the past and is subject to addiction, pain, illusion, and fear. The experiences of childhood conditioned the personality. Since most parenting was not totally adequate (no blame implied), the little self is stuck wanting what it did not get. This focus on the past of pain, deprivation, unmet dependency needs, abuse, etc., creates the split from the Higher Self.

You can begin to heal this split by connecting with your Inner Self in meditation, prayer, contemplation, journal writing, remembering your dreams, being in nature, and honoring and listening to your intuition. Reading self-help books and going to lectures on self-growth helps to expand your awareness. You may need a teacher or counselor for a while to facilitate your inner abilities. As you begin to trust your inner experiences more and more, you will allow this spiritual healing into your life.

As you go deeper and deeper with your healing, you will want to know the answers to such questions as, "Who am I?, Why am I here?, What is my purpose?, How do I live my life to the fullest?"

Unconditional love from Spirit is already pouring forth from the Source of your being to heal the pain, suffering, and isolation of you not loving yourself. You don't have to earn it, you need only accept it. Remember to LOVE YOURSELF from your Spiritual Self to truly heal low self-esteem.

As you heal yourself, you add peace to the collective consciousness of our world. World peace begins with you.

Final Affirmation

**I Take the Next Step for Me Today
to Grow Into My Full–Potential Self.**

SELF-ESTEEM BOOKS, TAPES, AND PRODUCTS
by Suzanne E. Harrill

Product	Price	Quantity	Total
Affirm Your Self Day by Day Book w/Daily Affirmations	$11.95		
Affirm Your Self Cassette	$10.95		
Self-Esteem Cards (for adults) Affirmation Cards w/Wooden Acorn	$9.95		
Seed Thoughts for Transformation (Unfolded)	$9.95		
366 Affirmations from Affirm Your Self (Folded in Plastic Box)	$19.95		
You Could Feel Good Book	$8.95		
Self-Esteem Curriculum Guide to use with You Could Feel Good	$19.95		
You Could Feel Good Three-hour Cassette Album	$19.95		
Building Self-Esteem Cassette One-hour Lecture	$10.95		
Empowering You to Love Yourself Book	$9.95		
Teaching Children Self-Esteem Video for Parents and Teachers	$19.95		
I am a Star! Children's Book	$6.95		
Children's Self-Esteem Cards with Star Eraser	$8.95		
The I Love the Earth Book with Colored Pencils	$3.95		
Empowering Teens to Build Self-Esteem Book	$8.95		
Wooden Acorns (each)	$1.00		
Star Erasers (each)	$1.00		
One copy each of Adult, Teen, & Child Self-Esteem Awareness Indicators Can be copied for teaching purposes	$1.00		
Sales Tax TX Residents Add 8.25%			
Shipping & Handling $2.50 for first item plus $0.75 each additional item			
Total			

Send this order form with your check to:
Innerworks Publishing, PO Box 270865, Houston, Texas 77277-0865, USA
Write for a free catalog.

Suzanne Harrill facilitates other people's growth through writing, teaching, and counseling.

Over the years, Suzanne has taught self-awareness classes, trainings, and workshops to many different groups of people—children, teens, college students, counselors and therapists, teachers, parents, adults in continuing education classes, and volunteers in non-profit organizations. She was on the Speakers' Bureau for the Mental Health Association in Houston for many years. She began her public speaking in 1981.

Suzanne Harrill has a master's degree in Education and is a former school teacher. Currently she is a Licensed Professional Counselor and a Licensed Marriage and Family Therapist. She has a business, Innerworks Counseling, where she has done private counseling since 1982. Through her business, she has self-published several books, tapes, and self-help products.

Presently, Suzanne is on the Board of Directors for the National Council for Self-Esteem and has helped start local chapters of this organization in Houston, Texas and Gillette, Wyoming. Suzanne is married and has three daughters.